Collective Thoughts

Poems by

Joyce Atkinson

A CIP catalogue record for this book is available from the British Library.

ISBN   1-84436-084-9

CLASSIFICATION: POETRY

Printed and bound in Great Britain.
First published in Great Britain in 2004 by
United Press Ltd
Admail 3735
London
EC1B 1JB
Tel: 0870 240 6190
Fax: 0870 240 6191
All Rights Reserved

Paper used in the production of books published by United Press comes only from sustainable forests.

www.unitedpress.co.uk

CONTENTS

BRAVE PEGGY

I thought, one day
I wish my back pain would go away
I did not know that arthritis could be this bad
Then, I remembered Peggy.
Peggy could only lie there in her bed
She could not raise her arms, or turn her head.
Neither could she wash herself or comb her hair.
Yet she spoke calmly, when I was there.
Her sister Joyce, was very sad,
To see poor Peggy suffer so.
She hand fed Peggy four times a day.
Then one day, our lovely Peggy passed away.
God in his mercy knew
She had been brave, until the last.
So he took her home, and in his arms, he held her fast.
Now, when I think my days are bad
I think of Peggy, and I say "I am still lucky,
I can do a lot of things for myself today."

THE KINGFISHER

Little gems, that's what I call them
For like a jewel, they seem to me
As I remember when I first saw one
Across the river, on a willow tree
As I crossed the bridge to school
On a lovely summer day,
How he glittered and he sparkled
Made me wish that I could stay
As I lingered for a while
He dived and came up with a fish
Was it for his lady friend
Or could it be his breakfast dish?
But I was just a child of nine
So I could no longer stay
But the memory has stayed with me.
Of that very special day
Last week, I saw a programme
Which was filmed for all to see,
It was named 'Halcyons of the River'
But he is still just Gem, to me.

I REMEMBER HER WELL

She had been a stunner in her day,
That, no one could deny
The men stopped work to stare at her,
Whenever she passed by.
Some whistled, others shouted,
She pretended to be shy,
But really she rather enjoyed this,
Being ignored made her want to cry.
She was a raven haired beauty,
The sort who stood out in a crowd.
She knew how to apply her make-up,
Without it making her look common or loud.
But each year, as she grew older,
Although no one else seemed to care,
She would look in her mirror each morning
Before she combed her hair
And the sight she would see,
Filled her full of disgust.
No one liked her any the less,
And her husband tried hard to convince her,
That she was a beauty yet.

GIVE ME TIME

First thing on a morning,
My eyes are both bright red.
First thing in the morning,
When I've just got out of bed.
So knowing it's too early,
For a poor old soul like me,
I climb back into bed,
Until I'm brought a cup of tea.
If I look in the mirror,
At the break of day
I can see how other people,
Would want to run away,
I haven't got my make-up on,
I'm not a pretty sight
And people who are squeamish
Could get an awful fright.
So if you're coming to visit me,
Please do come after ten,
for I'm wide awake
and have found time,
to put my face on, by then.

THE RIGHT SENSE OF VALUES

It matters not a jot, if you're well-dressed, or not
Or how you have styled your hair.
It matters not a jot, if you have a little spot
Or if your dress has got a tear.
It only matters how you spend your life
And how you spend each day.
What you say and do for others
That you meet along the way
This will really make a difference
To the way folk think of you
There may come a time, in later years
When you may need help too.
Just remember, when your time on earth
Is very nearly done
That folk will only remember you
For the good things you have done.

COLD COMFORT FARM

It was cold comfort farm, so the children said,
Whilst eating their breakfast and fresh out of bed
They sat round the table, with bacon and egg.
The Aga was glowing, with fire bright red.
But out of the window, the heat did escape
And they noticed their father come through the farm gate.
Dad had his coat on and was all muffled up
To face the outdoor world, the going was tough.
The birds needed water, the goats should be tethered.
You can't put it off, just because of bad weather.
He flung wider the window, to get to the tap.
The cold wind blew in creating a draught.
The children all wished they were snug in their beds
And could pull the bed-covers over their heads.
But dad said "look lively there's work to be done.
And a breath of fresh air never hurt anyone."

I'M FROM COUNTRY STOCK

I'm from country stock, it's plain to see
No lying in bed late for me
I have to be up at the crack of dawn,
To milk the goats on my father's farm.
Then there's swill to be mixed and pigs to be fed,
And whilst you folk are still in bed,
I'm out there soaking up the sun
Time enough to play when the work is done.
My appetite, it takes some beating
And by now a big breakfast I am seeking,
Ham and an egg, or maybe two
Served sunny side up, will do.
Then out again and I think I've heard,
The beautiful song, of some kind of bird,
It might be a blackbird, or it could be a thrush,
But these days, you don't see thrushes so much.
Oh, I wish he'd come closer, so that I can see,
But he seems so elusive, up there in that tree.
When I get up very early, in Spring,
I hear the dawn chorus, when all the birds sing.
And it gladdens my heart to be able to say
I'll be a country girl, to the end of my days.

A CORNISH SCENE

It was early July and I watched
The lightning flashing
Over the Cornish hills
It was a grand view
From a house perched
High on the hill, at Egloshayle,
I could appreciate the scene
Across the tops of houses.
A person scurried past
Glad to be almost home at last,
Where it was dry and cosy.
Oh, that I could paint!
I could have got this down on canvas.
But I remember it well.
Lightning flashed, way into the night,
And the thunder kept me awake.
Twice the power went off.
I did not mind, as
I was happy just to watch the sky.
I'll learn to paint, that's what I'll do!
Then my next experience
I can write about
And show you too.

SWEET MARY

Sweet Mary, always wore a smile,
Unless someone she loved was ill
Then she looked quite ill herself
And looked like, she should take a pill.
Mary worried constantly,
But she never worried about herself,
That was not Mary's way
She thought of other people,
Until her dying day.
Through life she had missed out on much.
That all her friends enjoyed.
She hadn't spent much time at school
And had rarely been out with boys.
In spite of this she was so good
At everything she had to do.
Often when I went to visit,
Nice smells would waft through.
Her dinners must have tasted good
And I always got a cup of tea.
Mary never once forgot
To enquire about me.
If she went out shopping,
When the frost was on the ground
She worried about old people,
Who she thought should not be out.
Although I knew, these same old folk
Were not much older than herself.
I'm sure God's saved a place for her.
A special place, close to his throne.
She won't be lonely any more
When her heavenly Father takes her home.

COURAGE

I read in a newspaper, only the other day
Of a man who went climbing,
Way out in the USA.
It's a story of great courage
Which I'd like to share with you
And I hope that you will pass it on
So that others can read it too.
A boulder fell and crushed his arm
He waited five days to be found
But when he looked like dying from thirst
A solution had to be found
So taking out his pen knife
He cut off his arm and it bled
So he made himself a tourniquet
And from that rock, he walked away.
How many of us, do you think
In a similar situation
Would have the courage to perform
Such a dangerous operation?

THE WAITING GAME

With patience, I sat and I waited
For friends bearing gifts to appear,
But the brilliant day, had driven them away
That was abundantly clear.

I sat and I waited and waited,
But again I waited in vain
For the weather was really atrocious
Who wants to turn out in the rain.

Then for the third night, once more I waited
All spruced up and ready to talk,
But they must have been watching Coronation Street,
Or taking the dog for a walk.

It really is very disheartening
When your neighbour in the next bed
Has a whole lot of visitors around her.
and you have a book instead.

On the fourth night, I'd given up expecting
My hair hadn't even been done,
When a nurse kindly popped her head round the door
And said, a visitor, your son!

THE STORM

The wind blew
It blew the leaves off the trees.
It blew the washing from the line.
Women held tight to their hats.
Plastic bags blew around,
Turning dogs into nervous wrecks
As if that was not enough
The rain came down.
Then, the wind grew stronger.
Warnings went out to tall vehicles,
To stay off the motorways.
Even the strongest birds could not compete.
The wind dictated which way they flew.
It worked up to eighty miles per hour.
The Humber bridge was closed to traffic.
Distress calls came in from boats at sea.
On the coast roads waves came high
Over the sea walls.
Then once more, all was calm.
In the aftermath, after the storm,
Emergency services were hard at work.
Men were out in full force
Mending fences, putting new tiles on roofs,
Manning cranes to remove trees
which had blown across roads.
Some trees had blown onto houses and cars.
A few people lost their lives
And a few more were injured.
Everyone was glad that it was all over,
And peace reigned once more.

THINK POSITIVE

Life is full of ups and downs
There's good days and there's bad
Some days are full of failures
Which you wish you'd never had.
But putting the past aside
And moving on, to pastures new,
Forgetting it ever happened,
Is the best thing you can do.
You can wake up feeling full of joy
Ready to start the day
Or alternatively, with gloomy thoughts
Which will not go away.
But if you're feeling negative
I've noticed this before
Those are the days, when all goes wrong
And you wonder, what you got up for.

IF ONLY

If you could live your life again.
Learning from mistakes, that you had made.
Passing useful knowledge on to others.
Finding all the things that you mislaid.
Doing things you missed along life's journey.
Making up for time that you had lost.
Thanking all the people who had helped you.
Being kinder to your mate and boss.
If you could spend more time with others,
Putting their needs before your own,
Yet, trying to remember at all times
That charity, really begins at home.
If only! But it's never known to happen.
So make the best of life, the first time round
And don't put off a kindness towards others
Do it, whilst you still have both feet on the ground.

GHOSTS

It was a dark and gloomy day
When the ghosts of York went prowling
From the Shambles and the Minster
You could hear the north wind howling.
The ghosts talked to each other
About times not long ago,
When icicles hung from the roofs
And the ground was covered in snow
They walked towards the city walls.
Hoping someone to scare
And they saw a lot of shoppers, but
No one noticed they were there
So, to draw attention to the fact
They rattled their chains about,
Now, no one seemed to linger
And a few did scream and shout.
But whether they thought it was safer indoors,
and a good deal warmer too.
Ghosts can walk through windows and door!
But maybe nobody knew.
Only on this occassion, the ghost did not follow
Enough fun today
They could go back tomorrow.

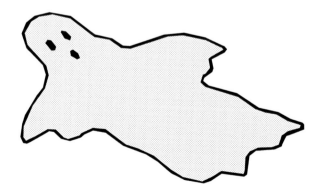

WHEN I WAS YOUNG

When shopping was done at Stroud's corner shop
And milk came in bottles each day
The milk man would pop his head round the door
and ask if you were okay
When children were timid of strangers
and stood by your side in a shop
Their meagre pocket money, only bought a lollipop
When summer air was clean air
and being outdoors was good
I'd spend many happy hours, helping dad saw firewood.
Each home had an open fireplace
Where on winter nights we sat
and pride of place would always go, to the family dog or cat.
When you grew your own potatoes
and children were seen and not heard.
Instead of loud disco music
You would hear the sweet song of a bird.
When bacon still tasted like meat from a pig
and your own entertainment, you made
This is the life I remember,
But this is the life we have lost.

THE WESTMINSTER CHIMES

In a field, amongst the rubbish,
Where my children went to play
Was a Westminster Chimes
That my father threw away.
It was very old and dirty
No one had the sense to see
It had been a thing of beauty
If restored, it still could be.
So I begged if I could take it,
And although it took all day
By evening it was shining,
All the dirt had come away.
Then my spouse he got it working
It is on our wall today.
What a shocking waste, it would have been
To throw that clock away.

DIFFERENT ATTITUDES

It is said to be a caring profession.
Admittedly a lot of doctors care.
But others are just in it for the money
And hardly even notice you are there.
By the time that you have had your consultation
This type of doctor's bored out of his mind
He can't wait to get rid of you
He makes it quite clear, that he's through
And wishes to get rid of all your kind.
The more you need to know, the less he tells you.
When you leave him, you are more worried than before.
But he's through the door and gone,
Just as quickly as he'd come
And his kind nurse shows you out through the door.
What a lot of us it seems when we most need them
Are at their mercy and must be treated in this way
Oh I wish that I could help, other people like myself
But all that I can do for them is pray.
It is no use to complain, they stick together
And who is prepared to listen to the likes of me.
If I held an influential position,
Or was young and blonde, I'm sure I'd make them see.
But I am past my prime and there is no pretending
The only thing that helps me to survive
Is the thought that others care
And good friends are always there.
It means a lot to know they're at my side.